Break Up
or
Make Up?

TOOLS FOR TOUGH
RELATIONSHIP DECISIONS

Rainah Davis

Published by: GC Simmons Publishing, Morrisville, North Carolina
Editing: Gerald Simmons, Cherie Graham, & Jennifer Eiland (Start Write, LLC)
Front Cover Design: Rainah Davis & Brittany Oliver
Back Cover Layout: Mainland Creative
Interior Layout: Erica Smith

ISBN-13: 978-0-9984271-3-3

Dedication

Relationships affect so many aspects of our lives, and it is my fervent hope for you that you would be able to break free from a destructive relationship or heal and mend one that just needs to be prioritized and given tender love and care. When I was walking through the valley of relationship death, God provided many people who guided, loved, and prayed me through it. I, therefore, dedicate this book to every single person facing a next to impossible relationship choice. Please know that, I wrote this book especially for you as you navigate your way through the valley of relationship decisions.

Preface:

My Story

In 2010, I faced the most difficult trial of my life. I accepted the failure of a desolate, miserable marriage and prepared myself and my four daughters for a move that was completely unexpected for them and utterly terrifying for me. After years of praying, fasting, and begging God to resurrect my dead relationship, I was finally ready to listen to the figurative thunderous "No" I felt as though I had heard from the Heavens.

Eight years later my only regret is that I didn't leave sooner. I am married to the man of my dreams, and have never been happier in my adult life. He is an exceptional husband, step-father, and son-in-law. He is super supportive of all my endeavors and he is my biggest cheerleader. He is also my toughest critic and always speaks the truth to me in love.

My life is a testimony that sometimes the path to a better life is being brave enough to stop settling for the present one. At the time I met my husband, I was a single mom with four daughters and had an extremely demanding job. However, we made time for one another and dated without wearing the masks that many people wear when they meet a prospective mate. We were open and honest about our past mistakes and our non-negotiables. I believe this is what makes our marriage continue to get better; we knew exactly who we were marrying. There were no surprises from each other, because we used our dating period to make all the tough decisions.

I believe that every relationship has a period where one or both of the individuals contemplate ending the relationship or continuing it. Healthy individuals take this period very seriously. They do not ignore the alarms that go off when their significant other commits a negative action. I named it the "break up or make up" period. This period is much easier to accurately assess if:

1- **You are still in the dating phase**

2- **You have not been physically intimate**

3- **You have not announced your undying love on social media**

4- You do not live with one another

5- You do not have children together

Once you have made a "public" commitment to each other, it can be more challenging to face your relationship woes. If you are married, have children, or live together it is more difficult to make a quality decision that is best for the both of you. As we progress, I will share more examples from my life. I pray that this books helps you to thoroughly assess your relationship and make a healthy decision. Alright, let's get started!

Table of Contents

Foreword

It's OK to quit! Now, I know you're shocked because you're not used to hearing words like that coming from a man who is extremely motivational. So generally the expectation from me is to always encourage you with familiar phrases such as:

"Keep going!"

"Don't stop!"

"Giving up is never an option!"

Although we are accustomed to those motivational messages, those words cannot be applied to every situation. Truthfully, one thing that I've learned is that sometimes you need to be motivated to let go. Everything that you try is not supposed to work.

In my life, I've learned that failure is often a good set up for significant success. It's true. So many people go through life in misery because they refuse to let go of something that they should have disconnected themselves from years ago.

Can you imagine just how many people are buried six feet under in the graveyard that could've achieved so much more than life, but because they were so motivated to keep going, or to keep pressing, they never walked away from something that was actually burdening them and not blessing them? Don't be that person!

In this book, Rainah Davis is going to give you divine instruction on how to, walk away from harmful and dysfunctional relationships the right way. For me, the most painful season of my life required making a tough relationship decision. I will never forget it. While most of my friends were married to the spouse of their dreams, I was in a relationship that turned my life into a living nightmare.

Honestly, I didn't see it at first, but when it was revealed to me, I was wise enough to begin to ask God for a way of escape. Please understand, it is not God's will for any of his children to go through life being used, abused or manipulated! That is actually the perfect will of the enemy.

Somewhere along the lines of training up a child, we've been taught from an early age that quitting should never be an option in life. Although those lessons are well-meaning, they often aren't explained in the context of relationships. Those lessons were not meant to extend into situations where individuals are being abused or mistreated. As a result, many people live their lives being taken advantage of in family/friend relationships, jobs, churches, and in marriages. This is where walking away is OK! For you or somebody you know, breaking up with a person who is making you miserable would actually be your greatest breakthrough!

The phrase "what God joined together let no man separate" is biblical. I want to be clear, I believe the Bible entirely. I have just learned that we must apply biblical truths accurately because if we are honest, every marriage or relationship that has been joined together, was not, in fact, joined together by God. Truthfully, every relationship in existence is not God's perfect will. While counseling couples, I have repeatedly stated that because this relationship is what "man has joined together" "man must now be separated" before both parties lose their minds and even possibly lose their lives.

Now, as bleak as breakups can be, I don't want to leave you with the idea that quitting is the only option when things aren't going so well. Jesus told us in John 16:33: "That in this world we would have trials and tribulations, but we should be of good cheer because he has already overcome."

This passage lets us know that we shouldn't expect every area of life to be perfect, but to expect that there will be ups and downs. Relationships are no different. Although trouble may arise, there also biblical and practical solutions that help turn an unhealthy relationship into a healthy one. I want you to be encouraged and know that even when the storms rage, they never last forever. Recognize that there is a difference between the experience of temporary turmoil and trouble that's designed to absolutely destroy you. God does give us the strength, wisdom, patience, and direction to overcome those temporary obstacles that emerge in relationships.

Realize that godly relationships do face attacks. When God connected you together with that incredibly unique one-of-kind mate, you can expect the enemy to attack your union. However, knowing that greater is He who is in "your relationship" than he that is in this world should give you confidence that together you can face any challenge and survive. This book was created to provide you with tools and tactics to assist you in strengthening your union in challenging seasons.

When I was in my terrible situation, my most fervent prayer was that God would create a way of escape for me to help me to get free from that experience. Let me tell you, God will do it! I know because He did it for me!

Unfortunately, the way that he blessed me to escape from the situation wasn't so pleasant. But in the end, I knew that it was all God. Today I can honestly say that I feel like the happiest man alive! I'm happily married to my best friend, I'm a proud father to a strong, healthy baby girl and I'm leading an international ministry that's impacting millions around the world. Guess what? The best part is that I'm free from the pain of my past heartbreak. My mind isn't cluttered with the thoughts of, "what of it happens again?" I refuse to let fear pollute my present or my future!

I'm fully healed from the struggles of yesterday, and I daily thank God for the new and exciting expectations that I have to grow in love, success, and wisdom with my family! This would never be possible if I didn't quit the negative, destructive, dysfunctional relationship. I am encouraging you and empowering you to QUIT what's killing you so that you can live your best life, with the right person and win!

~MARCUS GILL
FOUNDER AND CEO OF MARCUS GILL INTERNATIONAL,
MYRTLE BEACH, SC
EVANGELIST, AUTHOR AND SOCIAL MEDIA INFLUENCER

Introduction

I have been fortunate enough to survive all types of relationship woes described in this book (bad break-ups, separation, and divorce). I have also had the worthwhile experience of watching couples reconcile from these extremely harsh situations, as well. Mainly, for these reasons, I have written a follow-up to this guide called *The Shipwrecked Relationship*, written to help those individuals whose relationships did not survive.

In this book, we will suggest strategies to navigate the aftermath of the relationships' falling apart. First, however, I would like to address the people who are still hanging on by a thread in a severely challenging or troubled relationship. Unfortunately, most of us know people in these situations, and if you are one of the many individuals who has been "riding out" a see-saw/rollercoaster relationship battle and trying to decide whether to hang on or quit, I have written this book just for you.

State of Emergency

Do you remember the movie *Titanic*? This movie blockbuster, released in 1997, was a love story woven around the tragedy of the legendary and most luxurious ocean liner of its time. This occurrence was intensely shocking because the Titanic was supposed to be an "unsinkable" ship. The term "unsinkable" might have remained true if the ship had never hit an iceberg. The Titanic is very much like relationships in the 21st century.

Couples enter relationships believing that they are "unsinkable"—they truly believe that "love will conquer all" and that "myth," unfortunately, is the iceberg lurking in the sea of love.

As time passes, we find out that "love" really doesn't conquer all. We discover that making love relationships last requires persistent work. It also requires commitment and sacrifice from both people in the relationship to keep the flame of love burning brightly.

If you are reading this, it is highly likely that you and your partner have discovered just how fragile love is. Now that you have reached this critical realization, I want to give you some steps to assess how severe the damage is and to determine whether or not you and your significant other should try to make up or break up since the latter may be severely and unfortunately a possibility/reality. So, let's gear up and face the phases of the storm together.

Chapter 1

Face the Reality

Step One: Realize that you have been "hit."

Your relationship has figuratively hit an iceberg when one or more of these occurrences are happening on a regular basis:

1- The arguments are getting worse— (you used to argue rarely or occasionally, but now you have verbal disagreements regularly or almost daily).

If regular communication results in disagreement, arguments and/or insults, these apply ominously to your relationship. Often, couples who land here frequently started here to a lesser degree. You and your mate may never have communicated well, and the arguments intensified after engagement or marriage. Unfortunately, this type of relationship decline is common with mismatched or unequally yoked couples. However, the symptoms of incompatibility foretell the delayed, but inevitable death of an unhealthy relationship. When I say unhealthy I mean a number of things:

A- Unequally matched— (you want different things materialistically—one person wants to live in a mansion for parties, guests, and extended family and the other person wants a lovely townhome that has just enough space for the occupants) OR you want different things in life (one person wants the couple on a "career and business path," and the other wants to pursue a primarily "family path"—where family is first, and career is second). This divergence is going to cause a huge divide that eventually will lead to severe issues. Keep in mind that nothing is wrong with either objective; the problem arises when the couple lacks agreement on which path they should take collectively.

B- The relationship was rushed and the individuals never really got to know one another. Often, some couples end up together because of physical attraction and sexual activities are high on the couples' priority list while the consideration of emotional bonding and being sure that the two are truly compatible isn't as high on or even on the list at all. These couples can survive a long time off passion, attraction, and physical chemistry. Those attributes alone just are usually not enough to keep couples together for a significant amount of time nor does it usually result in a holistically healthy relationship.

C- The individuals in the couple do not like anyone else in their significant other's inner circle (this can extend to family, friends, or colleagues). If no one in the husband's family likes his wife's family (parents, siblings, cousins, etc.) that is going to be an uphill battle to fight. If the wife doesn't like any of her husband's former classmates, teammates, or fraternity brothers then, according to some counselors, if you don't enjoy any of the husband's friends, you might not like him. There are instances where people are friends with people who are opposites of themselves, but that mix is rare. Most of the time, you are friends based on the similarities, and the differences make the friendship more fun.

D- If you do like the members of your significant other's circle, but those individuals cause issues for your relationship, this too can lead to serious difficulty. One of the most significant challenges for couples is trying to remain close to people whose lives may be very different from theirs once they go from being single to married or from single to being in a serious, committed relationship. For example, if you are married but all your friends are single, they may not understand why you need to go home by a particular time, or they may not understand why you have to go home at all, depending on their values and what your crew's "norm" is. So, if you and your cousins have always gone clubbing and then go to the Waffle House and you typically make it home sometime around sunrise, your prospective spouse may not be okay with that, especially if he or she was unaware of this ritual before you became committed to one another or got married. Also, know, even if the individuals all like each other, if the external relationships negatively impact you and your significant other's relationship over an extended period of time, then the relationship could become significantly damaged.

2- If you are "speaking to one another" but not "communicating" with each other.

This may mean that, while you may not be arguing, the communication is strained, negative, or apathetic. Examples of this can be: frequent sarcasm, one or more of the parties feeling as if the other is not listening, negative body language or disrespectful behavior (such as: rolling eyes, sucking teeth, walking out while the person is still talking, or calling the other person out of his or her name, embarrassing him or her in front of others, or constant nagging). Keep in mind that it is entirely possible to speak to someone every day with no love, no care, or no real intimacy. If every interaction has become more of a neutral-feeling transaction rather than a loving or at least positive exchange, then the relationship is definitely in a bad state. You know you are reaching this point when you begin to feel that you are "on the outside looking in" to his or her life or when you begin to feel more like roommates than lovers/ spouses.

3- The (seemingly) smallest things cause WW III to break out between the two of you.

   A- You can hardly agree on anything

   B- Activities you used to enjoy with each other, you no longer enjoy.

C- When you try to remember what started the fight, you rarely can recall it because the smallest things set off major explosive arguments repeatedly.

4- Counseling does not help.

A- One or both of you refuse to go to counseling—or the worse outcome—

B- Counseling has actually made your situation worse.

If you agree to go to counseling and it doesn't positively affect your relationship, then normally, this outcome is a serious red flag. Here are a few suggestions to potentially achieve an effective outcome:

- Make sure you seek counsel from a qualified, non-biased third-party

Please Note:

A- I worked for non-profit and religious organizations settings for over 20 years, and unfortunately, not all clergy are skilled at counseling people experiencing marital difficulty.

B- Qualified counselors will tell you when your case is beyond their expertise. You should not go to counseling for years without having breakthroughs.

A FEW SUGGESTED QUALIFIERS FOR COUNSELORS

a- They have training and/or experience

b- They will not take sides (they can remain objective/this often excludes family and close friends)

*Most family members and friends have a hard time remaining objective even if they start out being objective, please keep this probability in mind.

C- They have marital experience—if there are some couples in your life that have good, solid marriages that you can both trust and be honest and transparent with, that experience may help you just as much as a certified professional. (Please note that there are counselors who do an exceptional job and have never been married. Just be careful because whether it is good, bad, or ugly, it is helpful if they have a degree of relationship experience. They should not be a novice at matters of the heart themselves [the exception would be a certified counselor who has education and training]—

this is still one to consider strongly—there are very few fields in which we trust people to advise us if they do not have hands-on experience in that area).

If a counselor or therapist who is qualified, is non-biased and is a non-family member does not help you, then you must seriously consider if the relationship can continue.

There is one other reason that you may need to seek counseling, and that is if there has been a soul hurt or an incident that robbed an individual of his or her self-esteem. Also if an individual has been "crushed" because of a crisis of faith in his or her religion or experiencing a lingering church hurt, then a pastor, rabbi, or priest may be the best person for you to talk to about the current situation. Past issues in our life can trigger future traumas. For example, if a family member was convicted for assaulting one of the individuals in a relationship and the convicted person is released from prison, seeing that person after his or her release from incarceration could cause an emotional instability in the impacted party. That is an issue that may need to be addressed in appropriate counseling or treatment. Also, if a spouse or significant other lost a parent because of an illness, death, or unexpected tragedy, the situation could cause unbearable pain in the affected partner, and it could impair a relationship if not addressed quickly and appropriately.

Now, as bad as these observations may seem, and yes, your relation(ship) has taken on a substantial amount of water, the water alone is not enough to submerge your vessel. The good news is that you still have time to get the water out, whether the "water" (threat) is drama, disagreement, confusion or any other communication issues, there is still time for you and your significant other to get back safely to shore. However, whether your ship remains afloat or begins to sink will be determined by what happens next.

Chapter 2
Quick Public Service Announcement

Before we proceed to the survival tips for moving past the current state of difficulty, I have to let you know that some situations are absolutely beyond counseling, whether the counseling is from a "seasoned" couple, certified professional, or clergyman. If you are in a relationship which involves physical, emotional, or psychological abuse, you need to leave the relationship immediately and get to a safe place. Abusers' inclination to abuse is likely to get worse over time. Many of us love those movies *Enough* with Jennifer Lopez and *What's Love Got To Do With It* (based on the life of Tina Turner) with Angela Bassett, but those women were the fortunate ones. Many abusers leave their victims slightly wounded, severely damaged mentally, emotionally, and physically. If you are in one of these situations, please do not take that chance that the abuser will come to himself or herself and "come to Jesus" (reform).

To help you, my reader, understand the severity of abuse, I have included some 2015 Domestic Violence Stats from the National Coalition Against Domestic Violence (ncadv.org):

- Every 9 seconds in the US, a woman is assaulted or beaten.

- On average, nearly 20 people per minute endure physical abuse by an intimate partner in the United States. During one year, this equates to more than 10 million women and men.

- 1 in 3 women and 1 in 4 men have been victims of [some form of] physical violence by an intimate partner within his or her lifetime.

- 1 in 5 women and 1 in 7 men have been victims of severe physical violence by an intimate partner in their lifetime.

- On a typical day, more than 20,000 phone calls are placed to domestic violence hotlines nationwide.

- The presence of a gun in a domestic violence situation increases the risk of homicide by 500%.

- Women between the ages of 18-24 are most commonly abused by an intimate partner.

- 19% of domestic violence involves a weapon.

- Domestic victimization is correlated with a higher rate of depression and suicidal behavior.

- Only 34% of people who are injured by intimate partners receive medical care for their injuries.

- 72% of all murder-suicides involve an intimate partner; 94% of the victims of these murder-suicides are female.

- 1 in 15 children are exposed to intimate partner violence each year, and 90% of these children are eyewitnesses to this violence.

- Victims of intimate partner violence lose a total of 8.0 million days of paid work each year.

- Between 21-60% of victims of intimate partner violence lose their jobs due to reasons stemming from the abuse.

- Women abused by their intimate partners are more vulnerable to contracting HIV or other STI's because of forced intercourse.

- Physical, mental, sexual, and reproductive health effects have been linked with intimate partner violence, including adolescent pregnancy, unintended pregnancy in general, miscarriage, stillbirth, intrauterine hemorrhage, nutritional deficiency, abdominal pain and other gastrointestinal problems, neurological disorders, chronic pain, disability, anxiety, and post-traumatic stress disorder (PTSD), as well as non-communicable diseases such as hypertension, cancer, and cardiovascular diseases.

- Victims of domestic violence are also at higher risk of developing addictions to alcohol, tobacco, or drugs.

- Studies suggest that there is a relationship between intimate partner violence and depression and suicidal behavior.

You can get more information, read the above list in its entirety to see statistics for every state in the U.S., and find additional resources to help you seek help on their site (acadv.org).

If this section applies to you, please permit me to close it with a prayer for every woman, man, or child who has been affected and is trying to survive life fraught with pain, shame and silence. I am aware that everyone reading this book may not believe in prayer, and if that is the case, please feel free to proceed to the next section; but for all others who know, as the old folks would say, "the words and the worth" of prayer, please join me in praying for yourself and for those others affected:

Dear Heavenly Father, I come to you this day on behalf of your daughters and sons who are being afflicted in relationships by people whom they love. I pray that you would break every chain that in binding them in these relationships that could lead to their harm or death. I pray that you would free their minds and release their hearts from fear. You have not given us the spirit of fear, but one of power, love and a sound mind. You loved us so much that you numbered the very hairs on our heads. You created us with a specific purpose in mind, and you will be with us each day until we can complete our destiny in you. We are asking for strength to leave the situations they are in; we are asking for provision and resources to make the necessary changes that are needed for each of your children to have life and have it more abundantly. We come against every attack of the enemy and rebuke it in your name, Jesus. We pray for peace, we pray for hope and we pray that faith will come alive within them right now. We are believing for your divine protection, and we believe that even though the situation looks impossible, things which are impossible with ordinary humans are possible with you. In Jesus' name, Amen.

Chapter 3

Survival Key #1:
Learn Positive Response Skills

N ow that we have made our relationship
Public Service Announcement, we are
back to our topic already in progress.
Next, I will share the keys you will need to unlock
the relational complexities currently wreaking
havoc in your life. I am calling them the Relationship Survival Keys. Here is the first one:

Key 1: RESPOND RIGHT:
Your response is everything.

Emotional responses will sink your ship. Emotion is something that every individual has the
ability to control, but for the masses, this remains
an extremely difficult task to do. If there is ever a
time to master "emotional responses," it is when

your relationship is in critical danger. There are three responses that are relationship "killers"— actually, there are many more, but for the sake of time, we will focus on three.

Uncontrolled Angry Responses

Anger will take the ship down quickly. If either of you is hot-headed, quick-tempered and/or is prone to speak without thinking, mastering this emotion is going to be an essential step in saving your relationship and getting the water out of your boat. Anger is so devastating that once it is unleashed, it is like landing 100 fighter jets on that same ship that is already taking on water. Can you imagine how fast the ship would sink? Well, that is the effect that anger has; it can be both powerful and extremely destructive, and so can water. If you are going to change how you deal with anger and frustration, you are going to need some new Response Skills. If you are reading this book and you are a Christian or are familiar with the Bible, you may have read the following scriptures we will use to help us illustrate and define the Response Skills.

James 3: 2-5 NKJV

For we all stumble in many things. If anyone does not stumble in word, he is a perfect man, able also to bridle the whole body. Indeed,[a] we put bits in horses' mouths that they may obey us, and we turn their whole body. Look also at ships: although they are so large and are driven by fierce winds, they are turned by a very small rudder wherever the pilot desires. Even so the tongue is a little member and boasts great things. See how great a forest a little fire kindles!

RESPONSE SKILL 1:
CONTROL YOUR TONGUE

This verse reminds us that no one is perfect, but the person who can control his or her tongue comes pretty close. It also describes how some tiny things have great power, such as the small bit that is placed in a horse's mouth and the rudder that is used by the ship's captain. The rudder itself is tiny in comparison to the ship, but it has the ability to turn the entire ship. Lastly, if you have ever seen the news coverage of a forest fire, you know that a small flame can destroy acres of trees! In the same way, one comment can change the course of your relationship forever. You must always be mindful of what you are saying to your spouse, how you are saying it and when you are saying it. There are things that you can say in good times that are devastating in the bad ones, and then there are some things that you should never say. If one of you tends to struggle in this area, you may want to try this next response skill:

RESPONSE SKILL 2:
GIVE A GENTLE ANSWER

> Proverbs 15:1 (AMP)
>
> A soft and gentle and thoughtful answer turns away wrath,
> But harsh and painful and careless words stir up anger.

One of the things that my husband says that he loves about me is that I respond well to him. Not only do I keep him from getting upset with me, but I also use calm answers to prevent him from becoming angry with others. I'll give you an example. One evening we were awakened by our neighbors ringing our doorbell repeatedly. The neighbor's visit was very unusual because we did not know them very well at all. So my husband went to the door and then came back in, took off his robe and house shoes and started getting dressed. His actions seemed weird because he was not scheduled to work that day.

He asked me to get up, to get dressed and to come outside with him; however, he would not tell me why. Now, on the inside, I was frustrated because I did not want to get up out of bed yet. I definitely did not want to go outside, but I did as he asked and followed him outside. Well, I could not believe my eyes. His car was practically unrecognizable! Our neighbor had witnessed a car from one the houses down the street run into my husband's car while it was parked in our driveway; the impact of which had been so hard, the entire impacted side was caved in! My husband was distraught, and to make matters worse, and the guy had fled the scene. If our neighbor had not come and told us what happened, we would not have known and would have had to be fully responsible for the damages.

When the police arrived, the guy who had damaged my husband's car confessed. As horrible as the entire encounter was, now my husband has a used car in mint condition, so all is well that ends well. The reason I am sharing this story is that my husband used to be a fighter (accomplished boxer) back in the day, and he wanted to punch out the guy. I gave him fifty reasons why that was not a good idea and made thirty of them comical. He told me that at that moment, he was so grateful for me because had he been with some of his ex's when something akin to this incident had happened, they would have talked him "mad" (angry and aggressive). But I used gentle answers to keep him calm, and all involved safe.

This approach also works when someone is responding angrily toward you. A person who will scream at you while you are remaining calm with him or her is probably not the best relationship choice for you. One of the reasons that this response skill is essential is that it connects to the next one:

RESPONSE SKILL 3:
Deal with anger accurately and quickly!

Ephesians 4: 26 (MSG)

Go ahead and be angry. You do well to be angry—but don't use your anger as fuel for revenge. And don't remain angry. Don't go to bed angry.

There is nothing wrong with anger itself. My husband had every reason to be angry with the guy who hit his car, but punching out the guy would not have repaired his car, nor would it have made the situation better. The matter would have gotten a great deal worse had the situation turned violent. So we have to deal with the cause of the problem so that our emotions do not go spiraling out of control. Then we also have to act fast (but not impulsively)!

When my husband started expressing his extreme frustration, I started talking to him immediately. I did not wait to see if he would calm down on his own. The scripture above also states that you should not stay angry. Another translation of that same verse says: "Don't let the sun go down on your wrath." This admonition implies that it is wise to deal with anger sooner rather than later because anger is a seed that does not produce fruit; it produces only weeds. If you plant enough "anger seed" in your relationship garden, those seeds will eventually grow into weeds that choke all of the life out of the beautiful things you can grow there. The next relationship killer that requires a new set of response skills is Depression.

Unlike anger, which takes the relationship down quickly, depression takes it down slowly. Depression is a relationship killer that lurks in the shadows. It goes away during parties and happy times, but it shows up during bad periods and timeframes of discontent. There are many reasons that depression emerges in someone's life. We will discuss a few chief causes and then explain the proper Response Skill to apply to that situation.

DEPRESSION CAUSE #1:

Unresolved issues in one or more past relationships.

This relationship killer often affects women. It is not that men do not experience depression, but it usually is expressed in anger instead of the intense, moody, melancholy states that women face. One of the reasons that depression rears its head is that the current failing relationship triggers a forgotten or buried pain that the individual has experienced and not obtained healing. Depending on the age and season of life, this intruder can set off feelings of despair and hopelessness causing the female of the couple to never be able to experience "happily ever after." Unfortunately, until healing truly takes place, individuals are prone to select the same type of mate repeatedly until the revelation occurs that he or she may not be the best significant other. Another cause for depression to occur is comparison. Often, women can get into the trap of comparing their mate to someone else's. Making comparisons can be deadly to your relationship for a couple of reasons:

A- Don't go by just the pictures…you don't know what is going on in anyone's else relationship. The image may look great in public or on social media, but just because the grass looks greener on the other side, does not mean that it is.

B- Don't get sad based on what others tell you about their relationship. Because, unfortunately, people lie! I have known women to be jealous of relationships that I know are not as great as the person is portraying her relationship to be.

DEPRESSION CAUSE #2:
Unresolved parental issues.

Men who have issues with one of their parents, such as an overprotective mom, a mother who abandoned or rejected the son for any reason, a father who was never there, or a father that was too busy often struggle with anger; that is one of the primary negative emotions expressed by men. Depression caused by a failed relationship does occur, but it is not often revealed that it is linked to a parent. (*Please note that I am not saying that men do not experience depression. However, in this section, I am only referring to emotions that are visible or have been verbally communicated).

One of the relationship issues that women often deal with is the reality of everyday life with her "flawed" Prince Charming. Women sometimes slip into despair because of the actuality of living with another flawed human being who never measures up to the fantasy created during the dating period. As little girls, we grow up playing with our dolls and plan hundreds of weddings between our Barbie and Ken dolls only to one day discover that the after-wedding-life struggle is real work; nothing like "every day" honeymoon life that we repeatedly reenact with the dolls.

One of the benefits of women who grew up with fathers (and sometimes brothers) is that they have firsthand knowledge of the realities of living with men. They know that there are both positives and negatives. Often, women who do not have these experiences can be very disappointed when it time to live with their spouse if they had not lived with males previously.

Fathers play a crucial role in how women respond to men, either positively, negatively or both.

Unfortunately, women raised without dads tend to be more prone to have identity and/or abandonment issues. When a conflict occurs, depending on the type, it can also cause these issues to surface. When the issues arise, often the response is one of depression or anger. Both anger and depression are negative behavioral responses that will eventually cause your relationship to sink. If you are going to survive the hit, you both are going to begin to respond more positively to each other immediately.

RESPONSE SKILL 4:
Get healed.

We discussed this a little earlier, but too often, people jump into relationships before taking the time to heal from hurts of the past. Whether issues lingering from childhood or a former relationship that went bad, if you don't heal from whichever of these is applicable, you will never be as successful in your relationship as you could be. Sometimes getting healed means developing better relationships with parents. Sometimes, it means forgiving people who have hurt you in the past. Often, it means analyzing why the past love relationships didn't work. It also often means asking other tough questions, such as:

- Why do I keep picking the same kind of guy/girl?

- Why am I attracted to guys/girls that...
  _____?

- What do I need in my next relationship that I did not get in this one?

It may be helpful for you to look at the "pros and cons" of every serious relationship you have had. If the majority of the "cons" are all the same, you may be unknowingly attracted to a personality type that looks good to you or seems right to you but is extremely bad and harmful to you.

If either you or your significant other fits into either of these categories, for each other you will have to put in extra work to make your relationship last because it is highly probable that one of you chose the other through your brokenness and not in your wholeness of self. If it is looking as if you two are not going to "make it," and you end the relationship, make sure you do not make the same mistake again. Take the time you need to assess yourself and the types of partners you have chosen. If you do go through this process, you will be on your way to selecting a suitable mate for yourself and increasing your chances for a healthy and happy future relationship.

Chapter 4

Survival Key #2: Adjust your Expectations

Key 2:
Adjusting and adequately managing your Expectations is critical.

The truth of the of the matter is that unrealistic expectations add more water to your relation (ship), and in most cases, the relationship did not get broken overnight, and it isn't going to get fixed overnight either. Both parties have to set healthy expectations and define and agree on what progress means individually and dually. Expectations are not an issue only for couples. Expectations are an issue for humans, irrespective of personal relationships. Nothing causes more drama than these circumstances: what you "thought a person was going to do" versus "what he or she does." It can be tough dealing with the realities of who you "thought a person was" versus "who he or she is;" or "what you think someone can do" versus "what the person is truly capable of doing." One of the most helpful relationship survival techniques you can ever learn is to adjust your expectations. Here's how you do it:

Accept the person for who he or she is
and not just the person that you want to see.

I'll give you an example. When I was younger, there was a Head and Shoulders shampoo commercial which warned: "You never get a second chance to make a first impression." Often, that commercial demonstrated how people treat their public interactions - like an audition for a role. In a sense, these encounters are just that. The person you are meeting is presenting himself or herself in the best possible light so that he or she will be chosen or accepted.

The issue is that no one can "live on stage" forever. A stage is a great place, but only for a short time. Entertainment is a billion-dollar industry, but movies and theater complexes are places we visit to see actors and singers; they are not places we live. At some point, everyone faces the reality of being who he or she uniquely is, and if you are a couple in trouble, you must be ready to come off stage, take off the mask, and show up as yourself.

After you present yourself "mask-less", then, the other person in the relationship must be willing to accept the "real you." If the two of you cannot accept each other for who you are, you are going to have a tremendously difficult time moving forward. We mentioned this earlier, but it bears repeating:

A-Do not compare.

President Theodore Roosevelt is known for the famous quote: "Comparison is the thief of joy." This statement has never been more true. In an era of social media and the trending concept of "couple goals," it is more critical than ever to accept your spouse or significant other for who he or she is. Please avoid the comparison trap at all costs. You cannot expect your spouse to be like anyone else's and because you are not living with those people 24 hours a day, you never know what anyone is really like behind closed doors. Therefore, make sure you are not comparing your relationship to that of someone else's. When you do, the fantasy created in your mind typically quickly morphs into unrealistic expectations.

B- Accept each other's flaws and limitations.

When my husband and I were dating, he wasn't huge on verbal displays of love. If you are familiar with *The Five Love Languages* book, then you know this terminology is also known as "words of affirmation." My husband told me that he may get better over time, but that I needed to decide on whether I could be with him with his limited ability in the "words of affirmation" category. I decided that I could be okay with it; I loved him and felt as though the other benefits I received from him far outweighed this one area. So I kept my expectations extremely low, and he has pleasantly surprised me.

He is more verbally affectionate than I ever imagined he would be! Now, this ended up being very satisfying because first, I accepted him the way he was and his limitations but also because he did not pretend to be someone who was super affectionate verbally while we were dating and then later we ended up fighting because "he changed." Often, the behaviors that we believe to have "changed" are the true dormant behaviors that had been suppressed to win the affection of our person of interest.

C-Manage Your Expectations for the Future

There is nothing sadder than a couple whose relationship fails because the two could not grow together over time. After accepting your significant other for who he or she is and accepting his or her flaws and limitations, you must also be prepared for change. If your wife is a stay-at-home mom and cooks full-course meals, and does all of the cooking and cleaning, that same exceptional wife may need some help from you if she returns to work and has a very demanding job.

If you have a husband who usually helps with the children every weekend but suddenly gets a new work schedule that requires him to work weekends, you will have to adjust your expectations of your spouse, based on the change that has occurred in his life. Life will constantly change. The only time everything will remain the same is when you die. All living organisms grow and change. You may run together when you are in your twenties, but those runs may turn into brisk walks in your sixties, depending on your health. If you can appropriately manage, adjust and re-adjust your expectations as life's changes come your way, you will be able to stand the tests of time as a couple.

Chapter 5

Serve and Protect

Survival Key #3:
Put Their Needs First

If you and your partner have decided that you are trying to make your relationship work, then you both should be going beyond the ordinary to make each other happy. You should be obsessed with meeting your partner's needs, and the other person should be obsessed with satisfying yours. In my relationship, I am continually amazed at how my husband serves me. He commutes three hours a day, six days a week, so that our girls (my biological and his step-daughters) do not have to change schools and so that I can be close to my parents and my oldest daughter's family, which includes our son-in-law and grandsons.

In addition to these accommodations, he checks on me before he drives home to make sure that we do not need anything from the store. Now, I am five minutes from the store, and often, I have told him that I will go, but because I am an entrepreneur and in school full time, his going to the store for me is a way that he supports me and serves me. He values my contributions and what I do for the house, so I reciprocate by making him breakfast every morning and by packing his lunch every day. Although he is completely capable of making his food, I make it for him. It is my pleasure to take care of him in this capacity because he takes such good care of me.

He makes time for us to do date nights weekly. However, because I know he is often exhausted from the commute, every once in a while, I will surprise him on a date night and do a "date night in." A "date night in" is where I have already cooked for him and have a movie set-up for us to watch so that we can enjoy each other's company at home. For him, this "sweetens the deal" because he doesn't have to get dressed up or leave the house. I do these particular things because I know that he needs to rest, in spite of his willingness to deny himself for me. That type of sacrifice is typical in a healthy relationship. If each of you is working overtime to make the other happy, the result is that you both end up happy!

Survival Key #4:
Protect Your Relationship from External Interference

Earlier we mentioned people as an external threat to your internal happiness. You must protect your relationship at all costs. You cannot let other people cause a fight between the two of you. If you two find yourself continually arguing about an external relationship (such as family members, friends, or co-workers), then you may have to limit or exclude them from your lives. If these people are your family, you often cannot completely cut off all contact with them, but you do need to make sure that your family members respect your mate.

Each member of the couple is obligated to defend his or her partner or spouse from his or her own family. I made sure that I chose a spouse that my family liked and that liked my family. However, I have been in relationships where the opposite was the case, and that period was a miserable one that I did not want to repeat. As a couple, you are an individual unit and you both must be determined not to let anyone disturb the peace of your union.

So negative external relationships should be dealt with before your relationship reaches engagement. If you have friends who don't like your spouse, you may have to cut ties with them or significantly reduce the time you see them because the marital relationship is a covenant that no one is supposed to break.

Special Cases:
Children and Blended Families

The one family entity you choose not to do anything about is children. You are not going to send your child away because he or she does not like your spouse, in the case of remarriage, or if you and the child's other biological parent were never married. However, I strongly recommend that you marry someone who understands or is willing to endure the challenges of blending a family. Sometimes, the children misbehave when the new person arrives hoping to drive him or her away. Sometimes, the children fear that the new (intruder in their eyes) person will take up too much of their parent's time or replace them in some way.

Blending families is much more of an art than a science, and each case is different. Nevertheless, it always requires arduous work, so you need to make sure that you choose a partner who is up to the task. After you have taken the time and care to select someone who is willing to love, steer and blend a family, it is critical to be sure that you never allow the children to disrespect your spouse. Now again, I am not talking about abuse allegations. You should always investigate any and all abuse claims because you must still choose to be safe than sorry. I am talking about the common "I don't have to listen to you" or "You can't tell me what to do" statements that can be universal declarations from minors regarding step-parents without explicit instructions and previously set expectations. Furthermore, you must protect your spouse, if need be, from the people who are a part of your circle and were a part of your life before his or her becoming a part of it.

Chapter 6
Recommit to the Relationship
(Become Friends, Lovers, & Life Partners)

Survival Key #5:
ESTABLISH A NEW COMMITMENT

Commitment is essential for anything that you are going to succeed in doing well. If you decide to go back to school, you are committing to being disciplined to the point of completing the tasks required to receive your degree. If you decide that you want to start a new business, then you may have to put your online streaming service on hold while you commit your extra time to hustle, grind and create the business of your dreams. In the same way, when you decide that you are going to commit, or in this case, recommit to your relationship, this decision mean that you are committing to some things, people and maybe even excursions, to give the relationship the tender love and care required to fix what has been broken. You may be wondering how exactly that works. Let me give you some suggestions:

A- FORGIVENESS

First, you must be willing to forgive. I know that may be difficult, depending on the challenges that you and your significant other may be facing. However, forgiveness is a non-negotiable for anyone with whom you are going to have a close, lasting, intimate relationship. I served a leader who described forgiveness in a phenomenal way. He described two types of forgiveness as "distant" and "intimate."

Well, in a distant forgiveness relationship, you forgive the person, but you are not necessarily forgetting the offense or giving the person an opportunity to hurt you again. This person has done something so offensive that he or she has lost the opportunity to be a part of your emotional inner circle. This individual will never again get a front row seat in your life. Nevertheless, you are choosing to forgive him or her so that you can have peace, not because he or she deserves it. I read a quote that said, "Being unwilling to forgive a person is the equivalent to drinking poison and waiting for the other person to die." It just is not going to happen. In this situation, you release the person for your own psychological and emotional well-being.

Forgiveness in an "intimate" relationship, however, is just not optional. When you hold an offense against someone with whom you are in a romantic relationship, the unforgiveness functions like a brick wall that just continually grows higher and higher until you cannot see forgiving the person any longer. Also, the brick wall that exists between the two of you makes it impossible for you to experience intimacy (you can't show physical affection through a brick wall that has grown high enough). The wall prevents meaningful conversations— you are trying to communicate, but a big thick, brick wall figuratively exists between you. The worst part is that the wall is not limited to your bedroom; it gets into the car with you as well. It, moreover, goes to church with you, and it is even present with you at dinner.

Forgiveness is a non-negotiable if you are going to stay together. This is especially true if the offense is adultery. You will never repair a relationship ripped by adultery without forgiveness. And it is true that the intimate forgiveness that my mentor described as "forgetting while remembering" must be granted. You remember it, but you cannot afford to dwell on it. Therefore, you make a conscious decision to forget it every day until eventually the bad memory has been replaced by so many good ones until it doesn't affect you the way that it did previously.

B- YOU MUST BE INTENTIONAL ABOUT PHYSICAL INTIMACY AND ROMANTIC EXPRESSIONS

For some couples, sex is never an issue, even when they are upset with each other. I know couples who claim that they are never angry enough not to sleep with their spouse. Now, as true as that might be now, if there is no romance, no emotional currency, that flame will eventually flicker out. Furthermore, you must be intentional about loving on your spouse emotionally as well as physically. Often, women are frustrated when their men touch them only when they are ready to make love; however, I know men who feel as though they may never have sex if they don't initiate it.

You must have honest conversations about what each of you needs. I worked in full-time ministry for a number of years; therefore, I learned a great deal about what men thought on a myriad of topics. I discovered that men love attention, being served, and having their egos stroked. I have met so many women who get upset when someone compliments their guys because they feel as if "he's going to get the big head" or become conceited. I never really understood that because often the thing that gets men into trouble with other women is that they meet or end up spending time with a woman who compliments them and is constantly telling him just how great he is.

In the same way, I know women who get entangled in emotional affairs with men who just listen to them talk or who do thoughtful things for them. These women often get caught up in these situations because they have men that spend very little time with them or pay them very little attention. These "blips" are just a few of other popular instances that I often hear about. At the end of the day, adultery is generally caused by one or more unmet needs. Any time you are in a relationship with an unfulfilled or unhappy person, you are in a danger zone. To summarize, be intentional about intimacy, romance and conversation.

C-BECOME FRIENDS

If you are fortunate, the person you are with started out as your best friend. He or she is the person who you told everything and hung out with the most. Next, you began spending more and more time together until you realized that you didn't want to ever be without him or her, because you missed this person when he or she was not nearby. You wanted to be around him or her all the time. My husband often tells me, "I like you, Rain; you're my friend." Now, he loves me too, but the "like" is more important. May I prove it to you?

You may have children that you always love, but you probably don't always like them, and that can be at any age. I have a grandson who is three months old and positively adorable, but when he refuses to sleep at night and my daughter looks as though she is on the verge of collapsing, he just isn't my favorite human at that moment! I just want him to go to sleep, as adorable as he is!

We will not even talk about my teenagers... well, you get my point. You can absolutely love someone who you really don't like that much and that is dangerous for a relationship. You need to go on dates. You need to hang out. You need to laugh about silly stuff, but it is important for you to commit to merely being friends. As a rule, if you can't commit to having a mere friendship, your relationship is in serious trouble.

D- BECOME LIFE PARTNERS, GROW TOGETHER.

Forty-eight percent of those who marry before the age of eighteen are likely to divorce within ten years, compared to twenty-five percent of those who marry after the age of twenty-five. This same source cites that each time an individual gets divorced, the odds increase that he or she will get divorced again:

- Forty-one percent of all first marriages end in divorce.

- Sixty percent of all second marriages end in divorce.

- Seventy-three percent of all third marriages end in divorce.

With the United States ranking with the sixth highest divorce rate country in the world, the numbers show that the more often we get married as a society, the worse we do at it. I believe the reason is that we do not learn from the mistakes in the first relationship, and that if you marry young and you do not choose a person you can grow with, you inevitably end up growing apart. Additionally, every relationship has the potential to leave you with more of everything…more kids, more debt, more emotionally baggage, more insecurity, more self-doubt, more bitterness and more distrust.

For this reason, it is essential to factor in compatibility and to make a good choice for yourself.

I was in a serious relationship that ended because of incompatibility. This man was in many respects admirable; however, we just wanted completely different things in life. He wanted to live in a mansion and drive luxury cars. I want to own multiple properties and businesses and drive a Toyota, maybe a Lexus, when I am completely out of debt. I don't want to own a property that is 10,000 square feet because I don't want to pay to heat and cool a place that is 10,000 square feet. That kind of expenditure is just not me. I found someone who agreed with my mindset, who is serious about building business, eliminating debt, retiring early, and leaving an inheritance to our large blended family of children.

I shared the stats about marriage so that you can seriously consider your marital decision. You shouldn't get married because your "maternity clock is ticking" or because you became pregnant (a whole different discussion). You definitely should not marry someone just because you have been in a relationship with him or her a long time. You need to evaluate why you have been in the relationship so long and the present quality of the relationship. It is so critical to make sure that you agree about the matters which are important to you both.

My husband was not married to either of his children's moms, so when we were married at ages thirty-eight and forty-two, we briefly discussed having a baby. Well, as much as we would have loved to produce a child that would be a symbol of our love and raise him or her "better" with all of the things we did not know as "younger" parents, we decided against it. First, we ended up with a grandbaby that we adored, and keeping him confirmed what one of my husband's cousins had told me years earlier when she had a baby in her late thirties, which was, "Having babies is a young woman's game." We laughed, but I never forgot that conversation. And when I was up walking the floor with my sick grandson, I quickly realized that I was unequivocally over my short-lived "baby-fever."

My husband ended up staying up with me most of the night, and we quickly agreed that we would both pass on our own "custom-made" baby life. However, we love being grandparents! And since we have been blessed to have our first grandchildren at relatively young ages, we have a good deal of energy to play with them and enjoy them. My point is that we agree that all the little people that we needed in our lives have been given to us by Denzel and Chynah, and the little ones who will come from our other children in the future.

Agreement is important. If you can agree about your life goals (career/housing/lifestyle) and life plans (retirement/financial planning/legacy building), you are on a promising track to being able to grow together. Growing together is important because life is going to happen whether you are ready for the challenge or not. If you are blessed to live, you are going to turn 40-50-60-70 whether you are ready or not. Life keeps going, and that is a great thing, because anything that is not growing is stagnant or dead. If you have found someone that you can truly commit to as a life partner, your relationship has a higher likelihood to succeed.

Chapter 7

Create a Relationship Plan for Success

One of the greatest challenges facing us as a society is the fact that we live in one of the most progressive and productive, yet challenging eras. We have more technology and more methods to communicate with each other than our ancestors, yet, communication is often more challenging than ever. In my graduate studies, I was assigned to read a book called *Elsewhere, U.S.A.* The subtitle of this book alone makes it worth the read: *How We Got from the Company Man, Family Dinners, and the Affluent Society to the Home Office, Blackberry Moms, and Economic Anxiety* (written by Dalton Conley).

The beginning of the book gripped my attention because of the author's description of his grandparents. He noted that his grandfather was away from his grandmother for eight to ten hours at work each day and did not speak to her again until he got home from work. I sat there in amazement because even though I was raised by a traditionalist and a Baby Boomer, I had never thought about "relationship communication life" before cell phones, messaging, and texting.

Now I began to think about how often couples communicate throughout the day via text messages, emails, or short calls, and if this change had made the relationship better or worse.

Therefore, I decided that we needed to create a Relationship Plan for Success. If a business wanted to hire you but told you that it did not believe in business or marketing plans, I hope that statement would make you reconsider taking the job. Yet, so many of us jump into relationships, serious commitments and marriages without a plan for the relationship. The very first thing that you must decide when you are starting a business is how your company is going to be classified. Is your business a sole proprietorship? Is it a partnership? Is it a corporation? The type of business you are is important, for it will determine not only how your business is defined, but how it is taxed, and how you must report it.

Often, I see people entering in relationships in which they do all the work, do all the planning, take all the risks and do all the communication. This relationship is like the sole proprietor. Nothing is wrong with this as a classification; however, you have all the responsibility, one hundred percent of it. That is an issue. If you do all the planning, all the paying and all the calling, you are in a relationship by yourself. That "solo flying" is not what a healthy relationship looks like. Each person in the relationship should contribute and share in the health and growth of the relationship.

I also know people who run their relationships like corporations. They have a board of directors who must weigh in and approve every decision. The board members can be childhood friends, fraternity/sorority brothers and sisters, parents, bosses, or children (youth and adult), but at any given time, these people have more authority in the relationship than the couple itself. This is dangerous. As a layout designer, I learned very quickly that one of the worst things to do is to be asked to design for a committee. It is virtually impossible to create one design which a group of people will all like. Each has different tastes and experiences, and all those considerations weigh in on each opinion - and you know what "they" say about opinions.

The best way to establish your relationship is as a partnership. Both partners are responsible for the success of the business. They may have different assignments, roles, and responsibilities, but both have equal interest in the entity being a success. Now that you realize that your relationship is a partnership, you need a relationship plan similar to a business plan. Also, you need a vision, mission, and goals for this relationship.

Our Vision

When my husband and I were married, we had a vision to live our lives in peaceful harmony through regular intimacy and affection, to alleviate debt and become financially free, to support each other through raising our young children, providing guidance to our adult children, and being jointly committed to looking after our parents as they grow older.

Our Mission/Goals

We agreed to support each other's dreams through career, continuing education and entrepreneurship; to work together to create revenue streams that would allow us to retire in our late fifties/early sixties; to attend to each other's needs emotionally and physically; to create revenue streams that would create financial legacy that we could leave to our children through capital, real estate investments/purchases/revenues and book royalties; and to be an example of a loving Christian couple who values God first, each other second, and then our family. For us, everything else falls after these three. Next, you should have a:

Strategic Communication & Action Plan
(Includes Suggested Homework-Reading List)

For us, it is very simple; yours may be more in-depth:

1- We listen completely before interrupting or responding. (We listen to understand and not just to respond).

2- We communicate consistently, yet respectfully. (We know each other's schedules, so that awareness prevents us from interrupting the other during work or scheduled events).

3- We know each other's primary forms of communication and check in with the other person when we have to communicate in a secondary format to be sure that the other one has received the information. (My husband does not read my emails unless he is expecting something from me, so if I send him something unexpectedly, I text him to be sure that he receives it).

4- Social Media! You need to know what is acceptable to be shared on social networks. You need to know how your significant other feels about you "connecting" with past friends, loves, etc. on social networks. Failure to communicate these parameters can create a major issue so it should be a part of your *Couples' Communication plan.*

5- Create a Couples' Action Plan. After making sure that your communication plan is solid, you need to make sure that you "divorce-proof" your marriage by creating an action plan which generates guaranteed happiness in your relationships. In order for you to do this successfully, I highly recommend that you read the *Five Love Languages* by Gary Chapman and *His Needs, Her Needs* by Willard Harley Jr. These books are not new. You can order a used copy online or download to your E-reader You have come this far to save your relationship, you might as well go all the way.

6- If you have experienced infidelity, I recommend the book *Torn Asunder* by Dave Carder. Although this is an old book, it is still my favorite work which deals with this disquieting and heart-wrenching topic. Infidelity requires an entirely different playbook to heal and recover effectively because the violation is so personal and traumatic. Relationship columnist Amy Chan described her pain in a *Huffington* blog post:

> *"Regardless of the support from friends and family during such a time, I felt terribly alone. To have your trust breached and your heart so wounded feels like there is a dark cloud of misery that follows you everywhere you go. It's with you no matter how you try to distract yourself. Even in sleep you cannot escape, as pain haunts you in the form of nightmares. You feel trapped, because there is nothing you can say or do to make it go away."*

Chan's description is so vividly accurate. I personally have survived being in relationships with serial cheaters, and I cannot think of too many things more crushing to the heart and soul as an unfaithful spouse or significant other. For that reason, if your relationship is suffering from the fallout of an affair, you have some serious decisions to make if you are going to stay together.

You will need to carefully and strategically move forward in order to heal and recover. The *Torn Asunder* book is really an amazing read for anyone working through extramarital affairs (physical or emotional).

Create Couple Holidays

Many people plan family vacations and I think that is wise, for there should be a time where you connect with your immediate, and even extended family, if feasible. Strength and unity are established when families spend time unplugged, sharing, and loving on one another. However, this sharing should not take the place of your "Couple" Holidays. Moreover, some days should automatically be on this "time-together" list:

1- YOUR ANNIVERSARY (Now this can be one or more days):

- The date you met
- The date on which you became engaged
- The date you first said, "I love you."
- The date you "recommitted" your love to one another
- Some other date that is significant to only the two of you

2- YOUR COUPLE VACATION TIME

You can create your vacation around one of the days in #1, or if you were married at a time that is difficult to celebrate because you have children who were born on the same day, or it is on another holiday, you can select another time of the year or another day to celebrate. Jason and I were married in early May, and because our anniversary often falls on Mother's Day weekend, we rarely celebrate our anniversary on that weekend.

3- AGREE ON OTHER SPECIAL DAYS

- Are birthdays to be celebrated with the family? As a couple? Individually? With friends? Or a combination?

- Are some birthdays more important to one spouse than the other? Is turning thirty a super huge deal to one person, where he or she would expect a party with all the bells and whistles, while the other person just wants to have a quiet dinner and a romantic walk on the beach? You should know how your significant other feels about "milestone birthdays" so that you can plan to celebrate him or her accordingly.

- What are the expectations regarding

family birthdays, including in-laws and children (this is especially important for blended families). Finally, you want to create a:

LIFE SUCCESS PLAN

Each person should sit down and write out his or her own Life Success Plan, an outline of what success looks like for the individual. The truth is that you will never be able to create success collectively if you don't know what success looks like for yourself as an individual. So many couples are in trouble because the other person was waiting for a spouse to "complete" them. Unfortunately, that kind of serendipity only results in happy endings in the movies. The trouble with that is you need to be complete and whole within yourself before linking yourself to another person.

One of the best aspects of getting married or remarried later in life is that you generally have a better idea of who you are and what you want. Usually, you are beyond the pretending stage, and you have learned the pitfalls of showing up on the dates while wearing the mask. If you have taken the time to properly heal from your heartbreaks, then you have owned the mistakes that were yours. You understand your strengths and your weaknesses, and you are committed to breaking the cycle of committing to a relationship that makes you worse instead of better, or one that accentuates your weaknesses instead of highlighting your strengths. I have been blessed to marry someone who does that; however, it took a "minute." I went through some rough years, before I owned my crap, healed, and decided to make a better relationship choice for myself.

Once you have created your own Life Success Plan, you can exchange notes and then create the Collective-Couple Life Plan that should align with your vision, mission, and goals discussed in the beginning of this chapter. Successful completion of this exercise will go a long way toward helping you to become exceptional life partners to one another. I confess that this chapter has a lot of steps, suggestions, and recommendations. You don't have to do any of these things, but I suggest that you try a few of them and see what happens. If you are reading a book that is helping you decide whether to fix or nix your relationship, you don't have a lot to lose.

I was married at eighteen and divorced by twenty. I was remarried at twenty-five and divorced again by thirty-four. I took the time to heal and admit to my faults in the relationships. I invested this time because I learned that in life when you fail a test, you have to take it again. Finally, I became sick of failing the relationship test. And I can say, that taking the time to heal and recognize the type of man that I was attracted to versus the type of man I needed was one of the biggest and most important breakthroughs for me.

I have lived in "relationship misery" and I have experienced relationship bliss. Now, I don't want to mislead you to believe that every day with my spouse is sunshine and rainbows. There are days when I get on his nerves and vice versa, but the good times always outweigh the bad. That is what I want for you, and that is why I took the time to write this book.

Chapter 8

Connect to a Power Source

I am Christian, and I believe in God. No matter who you believe in, I suggest that you tap into a higher power, because when you are weak, you need to be able to rely on someone far greater than yourself. When I look back at how I survived my past failed relationships, I realized that it was prayer, praise, worship, and the power of the Almighty God which powered me through the turbulent days of my life. In our humanity, we are all weak, we get weary, we get tempted, and left to our own devices, we will become selfish and choose our wants, needs, and desires over that of our spouse or significant other. Nevertheless, the reality is that it is better to give than to receive.

Being connected to God will help you choose the best person to give your help. Becoming a giver rather than a taker will make you a better person and elevate your relationship to another level. At the end of the day, you can try to fight this battle on your own, but trust me, it is way more difficult to do than trusting, relying, and depending on someone who created you and designed you with a specific purpose in mind. I want to encourage you to consider making God the head of your life. It is significantly easier "to do all things" (Phil. 4:13) with supernatural strength.

The statements which follow are extremely true if you have ever been in a relationship that made you feel as though you wanted to die or kill. Neither is a healthy state of being, and you are urged to do everything within your power not to repeat that type of relationship. You need wisdom; you need practical guidance and good relationship examples. I strongly suggest that you become a part of a church which has a good, healthy marriage ministry or a marriage support group that has seasoned couples leading it, couples who have survived some storms themselves.

A Prayer for You

Dear Heavenly Father,

Before we ask you for a thing, we just want to say, "Thank you." We praise You for everything that You have done and for the things that You are working out for our good behind the scenes. We thank You for causing all things to work out for our good because we love You and are called according to your purpose. We ask that You forgive us for every time we have ignored the signs that You have given us to walk away from a relationship that was never in Your will. We also ask forgiveness for not walking in love, grace, mercy, and tenderness for the special person You created and sent for us to love, but that we mistreated.

I pray now that for each couple that has decided it needs to break up, that You be with them as they mourn the relationship. We ask that You protect them from social media backlash and from the negativity of others. We ask that You bless them with a suitable mate for him or her. We know that You created Eve specifically for Adam and that You are able to give us a mate specifically suited for us. I am a witness, God, because You did it for me, and I know that You can do it for each reader.

I also pray for every couple who has decided to stay together. I pray Your covenant blessing upon them. I pray that they are compatible in every way. I pray that they have supernatural agreement. I pray that they experience overflowing love and respect for each other. I pray that You bless their love, affection, and intimacy and that each of them would desire only each other the rest of their lives. I pray that You bless the heart that is struggling with forgiveness. Bless them so mightily that they want to freely forgive because they experience the blessing of your forgiveness.

Finally, I pray that any individual not walking with You, has decided that he or she wants to receive You today into his or her heart as Lord and Savior. I pray that he or she will find a good church home, with a true Pastor filled with integrity and humility and blessed with an amazing church family. Keep them, protect them and bless them exceeding abundantly more than they ever imagined possible, in Your mighty and precious name.

Amen.

Bonus: Chapter 9
Special Situations

Earlier in the book we mentioned that abuse was not an issue that you could really work through. Abuse in any form is an automatic reason to sever a relationship as soon and safely as you can. There are some other instances that are worthy of an honorable mention. These issues didn't warrant an entire chapter of their own, but I believe that I should mention them.

ADDICTION

NARCISM

EXCESSIVE IMMATURITY

ADULTERY (MULTIPLE ACTS)

DISORDERS

MANIPULATION

GAMBLING

OVERSPENDING

COMPULSIVE LYING

PORNOGRAPHY

Relationships that are in trouble due to one or more of the topics on this list, typically stay in trouble without some type of aggressive intervention. Moreover, without outside help, these issues tend to escalate exponentially. One of the reasons is that committing one of these issues produces a snowball effect of added negative behaviors.

For example, an individual that has a gambling issue may start working extra hours to pay off a debt. His or her spouse may confront them that there is no evidence of the "extra hours" in the finances. This may lead to the gambler compulsively lying about where the money is going, which eventually would catch up to the gambler over time. This, in turn, may lead to excessive arguments between the couple which could leave room for one or both partners to have an affair. The affair could lead to overspending due to buying gifts for the third party, paying for rendezvous and meals.

Although this example may seem extreme, these are the types of "snowball behaviors" that can occur when addictive behaviors go unchecked. If you are in a relationship that is experiencing one of these special circumstances, please know that the first step is facing reality. You must understand that your significant other is not going to get better with help. If you are the affected party, you must take an honest look at your situation and be ready to make some significant changes.

Next, you must understand that there is no love without self-love. I am not talking about being **selfish.** The Bible explains that you must love your neighbor as you love yourself; therefore, loving "you" is critical, crucial and key. Self-love is placing the mask on yourself, before attempting to administer care to your loved one. This involves valuing your peace and saying "no" drama. My sister-in-law once gave me some valuable advice. She said, "I don't care who it is, refuse to let yourself get comfortable in another person's chaos." Even though I did not heed them immediately, over time, I begin to make changes that permitted me to break from the cycles of drama that I was experiencing.

Also, you must understand and accept the premise of "free will." As a Christian, I believe in an all-powerful God; however, God even yields to the free will of an individual. There is no love without choice, and God created us to be able to choose between life and death, as well as blesses and curses. In the same way, our loved ones make choices that we cannot fix or control. One of the greatest tragedies, is a person who loses himself or herself, who cares more about another individual's success and happiness than that person does.

I want to give you permission to release yourself from the "Savior" complex. Whether you believe in the resurrection or not, one thing is clear, there is only one Jesus who was died on the cross for the sins of the world, and thankfully, you nor I were given that assignment. So rest easy and know that it is not your "job" to save or fix the afflicted person. However, it is your job to apply tough love when needed. Tough love means that you stop the inclination to save, rescue, or enable the person. If you give money to an addict, you cannot claim yourself as a victim when they spend your money on drugs. Addicted individuals spend money on drugs, without rehabilitation, that will continue to be the case. Now tough love still provides an avenue for you to **help**. You can assist them with getting counseling or treatment. That is the healthiest role you can play for someone battling a cycle of addiction; otherwise, you will get sucked in to the manipulation and dysfunction.

Lastly, do not be afraid to make a hard choice. This may involve a complete life overhaul such as relocation, separation, or divorce. You may have to take some personal, alone time to assess your part in the cycle. It may require you to ask yourself some tough questions:

- *Why am I a willing participant in a relationship that is toxic for me?*

- *Why do I continue to select this type of mate for myself?*

- *How would my life be better if I was no longer in this relationship?*

- *Can I stay with this person and support them through counseling or rehab and apply healthy boundaries?*

In conclusion, if any of these issues apply to you, I would like to encourage you to seek an early intervention. Many individuals wait until it is too late to reach out for help.

Final Thoughts

Relationships are amazing when both people are committed to putting in the work to keep it healthy and strong. Compatibility is important, but staying together through all of the issues and challenges of life, can be much harder than coming together. In a day and age where relationships are openly displayed on social media through the lens of #relationshipgoals, it is even more important to make sure that you are not just staying with the person to "save face."

I have a good friend who knew he should not marry his ex-wife, but they had a child together and had been in a relationship for nine years. Out of all of their family and friends, only one person told them that they should not get married. Everyone else was sure it would work because they had been together so long.

However, what the friends and family did not know is that the couple argued all of the time. The guy would get so angry in the course of their fights that he would rip the doors off the hinges! Now, because he was handy and could fix them, no one ever knew. Three short years later the couple divorced. The issues that were not faced during their extended courtship and engagement surfaced very quickly once the two were under one roof on a daily basis.

My husband has taught me that people tell you everything that you need to know about them if you pay attention. He says even when a new person in your life is wearing a mask, if you pay attention, they slide it to the side from time to time and their true essence comes oozing out.

It is my prayer that you will not stay in a bad relationship too long. Whether it is a bad relationship that needs to be terminated or one that needs to be fixed, I hope that the information on these pages is helpful in helping you get closer to your own personal happily ever after!

I am cheering for you!

Rainah

Acknowledgements

First, I want to give thanks to God. It is in Him that I live, move and have my being. I exist only because of His mercy, goodness, grace, and forgiveness. I am a living witness that He doesn't treat us as our sins deserve, and that He will allow you to truly not look like what you have been through! He will let you go through the fire, but let you come out without a hint of smoke! That is truly my testimony.

Next, I want to thank my husband, Jason. He truly is my "happily ever after." Without a shadow of a doubt, I can say that I love him as much today as when we met. He is an amazing husband, father, friend, lover, and life partner. My life is sweeter with him in it.

I would not be here without my parents. Gerald and Ruby Simmons are two of the most loving and supporting parents in the entire world. They have shown all their children how to weather the storms of life and come out better, stronger and more loving on the other side.

I would like to thank my children for sharing me with my laptop and the people that God has assigned me to reach. My prayer for each of you—Chynah (Denzel), Rubie, Amirah, Adiyah, Braxton, and Jamera is that God will bless you with beautiful, strong and healthy relationships.

I am praying for each of you, and I love you all.

Your wife, daughter and mother

Additional Information

BOOKING
Rainah Davis is available for:
webinars, seminars, retreats, and conferences.

For booking, please contact:
rainah@rainahdavis.com

BULK BOOK ORDER DISCOUNTS
If you are interested in using this book for
a group study, you can purchase the book in bulk
at a group discount rate.

For bulk book orders, please contact:
sales@booksbyrainah.com